TRACKING

SEA MONSTERS, BIGFOOT, AND OTHER LEGENDARY BEASTS

BY NEL YOMTOV

Consultant:
Dr. Andrew Nichols
Director of the
American Institute of Parapsychology
Thomasville, Georgia

CAPSTONE PRESS
a capstone imprint

Velocity is published by Capstone Press,
151 Good Counsel Drive, P.O. Box 669, Mankato, Minnesota 56002.
www.capstonepub.com

Books published by Capstone Press are manufactured with paper containing at least 10 percent post-consumer waste.

Library of Congress Cataloging-in-Publication Data
Yomtov, Nelson.
 Tracking sea monsters, Bigfoot, and other legendary beasts / by Nel Yomtov.
     p. cm.—(Velocity. Unexplained phenomena)
 Summary: "Covers the search for animals that may or may not exist, including evidence for and against the existence of cryptids"—Provided by publisher.
 Includes bibliographical references and index.
 ISBN 978-1-4296-4817-2 (library binding)
 1. Monsters—Juvenile literature. 2. Animals, Mythical—Juvenile literature. 3. Animals—Folklore.—Juvenile literature. I. Title.
 GR825.Y66 2011
 398.24'54—dc22   2010036929

* The author dedicates this book to his "monster"-ously good buddy, Kevin Somers.

Editorial Credits
Mandy Robbins, editor; Matt Bruning, designer; Marcie Spence, media researcher;
     Laura Manthe, production specialist

Photo Credits
Alamy Images: Mary Evans Picture Library, 19; AP Images: Eric Gay, 10 (bottom left), Farmers Museum, HO, 43 (top); Burlintonnews.net, 38-39 (top); Courtesy of the Peabody Museum of Archaeology and Ethnology, Harvard University, 42 (mermaid); Fortean Picture Library: 9, 11 (bottom), 13, 14 (right), 15 (left), 17 (Yeti), 25, 35 (drawing), 36 (top), 40; Getty Images Inc.: Ministry of Fisheries, 31 (bottom); iStockphoto: demarfa, 8 (top), GlobalP, 4 (sloth), JoeLena, 20 (dinosaur), nilky, 5, 37 (top); twilightproductions, 4 (bigfoot), 12 (bigfoot); Shutterstock: akva, 42 (ticket), Anatoli Styf, 17 (footprints), Andrei Verner, 6 (bottom), 30 (top right), Andrejs Pidjass, cover (wave breaking), 29 (water), andrej pol, cover (sea wave), Andy Z. 34 (owl), Anton Balazh, 30 (bottom left), 41 (Earth), ARENA Creative, 26 (middle), 31 (top), AridOcean, 26 (top), Bork, 4 (teeth), 19 (teeth), broukoid, 11 (ufos), carroteater, 10 (film), Chen Ping Hung (design element), clearviewstock, 41 (stars), Condor 36, 39 (bottom), Dani Simmonds, 38 (bottom), Darko Kovaceric, 7 (top left), Denis Nata, 17 (tape measure), Denis Pepin, 11 (top right), Dennis Donohue, 35 (bottom), dicogm, 11 (flag), dusan964, 34 (raven), DY Dream, 37 (bottom), eAlisa, 34 (feathers), Eric Isselee, 18 (bottom middle and bottom right), 23 (seal), Evlakhov Valeriy, 26 (bottom), Excellent backgrounds HERE (design element), Faiz Zalxi, 33, Francois Etienne du Plessis, 6 (left), Francois Loubser, 45 (middle left), Galyna Andrushko, 16-17 (mountain), George Lamson, 6 (middle left), gracious_tiger, 44 (bottom), Grauvision, 43 (bottom right), hfng, 9 (circles), HomeStudio, 35 (pencil), hpf (design element), hvoya, 34 (top), Ilja Masik, 44 (top left), illusionstudio, (design element), irabel8, cover (breaking wave), James Steidl, cover (ship), 28, javarman (design element), JCElv, 22, Jiri "Tashi" Vondracek, 32 (forest), Kevin Bassie, (design element), Kuzma, cover (sea), L. Kragt Bakker, 44 (top right), Laila R, 45 (middle right), Lars Christensen, 12 (foot), livestock images, 27 (bottom), loannis loannou, 4 (map), 26 (map), Lukiyanove Natalia/frenta, 30 (top left), Map Resources, 14 (left), Matt Ragen, 24 (bottom), maxstockphoto, 33 (top right), michaeljung, cover (wave), Milos Luzanin, 39–40 (frame), mmaxer, 33 (top left), Nailia Schwarz, 32 (top), nicemonkey (design element), olly, 24 (top), Osa, 43 (bottom left), picsfive, 35 (notebook), PJF, 32 (car), pollockg, 15 (right), Popov Maxim Viktorovich, 36 (bottom), QQ7, 34 (bottom), Ralf Juergen Kraft, 23 (Nessie), 45 (top), Rosie Piter, (design element), Sailorr, 4 (octopus), Sam DCruz, 27 (middle), sinephot, 18 (top), Slavolijub Pantelic, 17 (ice), Snowshill, 6¬7 (fossil), szefei, 20 (bottom), tepic, 6 (middle right), 45 (bottom), Tischenko Irina, 27 (water), Ultrashock, 18 (bottom left), Vaclav Volrab, 6 (right), 8 (right), Viktor Gmyria, 7 (top right), W. Scott, cover (tentacle), 29 (tentacle), WebStudio24h (water), worldswildlifewonders, 21, Zaichenko Olga, 42 (newspaper).

Printed in the United Staes of America in Stevens Point, Wisconsin.

072011   006313R

TABLE OF CONTENTS

CHAPTER 1

ON THE TRAIL OF
HIDDEN ANIMALS

BIGFOOT

Imagine walking on a path along a lake. You hear a loud roar. You look up and are amazed by what you see. It's the neck and head of a huge dinosaur-like creature rising from the water.

KRAKEN

Or perhaps you're on a camping trip when you hear a rustling in the bushes. You move closer to check it out. Unbelievably, a 10–foot (3–meter)–tall hairy beast growls and runs off into the woods. Have you just seen bigfoot? Is it possible that creatures like this really exist?

MAPINGUARY

Come along on a search for monsters around the world. Travel to South America to look for the fierce chupacabra. Then journey to Scotland in search of the legendary Loch Ness monster. Our quest will even take us to Africa to hunt the fearsome mokele-mbembe. Get ready for an unforgettable adventure in search of odd and freaky creatures!

CRYPTID SIGHTINGS

land creatures sea creatures flying creatures

KONGAMATO

Cryptids are animals that have been reported to exist, but no clear proof of their existence has been shown. People have reported seeing them on land, in water, and in the sky. Keep your eyes peeled, and maybe you'll spot one too.

species	a group of animals or plants that share common characteristics

CRYPTID HUNTERS

Cryptozoologists are researchers who study cryptids. They gather local myths and folklore about unusual creatures. They speak to people who say they have seen one. These stories and reports provide important information about how an animal may look and behave.

FACT

Often local people had been telling stories of a mysterious creature many years before scientists discovered the animal.

CRYPTID DISCOVERIES

Many scientists believe cryptozoology depends too much on folklore and witnesses to be scientific. However, some important discoveries have given cryptozoology more credibility.

1870S

The mythical sea monster the kraken is proven to be the very real giant squid.

Cryptozoologists also search for creatures themselves. They try to photograph animals and make sound and video recordings of them. They also study the fossils of creatures that are similar to the animal they are hunting. This research can help them know if the animal is a relative of a long-dead creature.

FACT

The word "cryptozoology" comes from the Greek words *kryptos*, *zoon*, and *logos*. *Kryptos* means hidden. *Zoon* means animal. And *logos* means study or knowledge.

1912

The komodo dragon, a lizard once thought to be a myth, is found in Indonesia.

2006

A hunter in Canada shoots a bear that is a cross between a polar bear and a grizzly bear.

CHAPTER 2

THINGS THAT GO BUMP
IN THE NIGHT

Height: 3 to 5 feet (0.9 to 1.5 m)

Features: sharp claws; sharp teeth; glowing red eyes

CHUPACABRA

In 1995 people in the small town of Orocovis, Puerto Rico, discovered an awful sight. Eight sheep had been killed. The bodies had **puncture** wounds, and there was no blood left in them.

Months later, horrified people in Canóvanas, Puerto Rico, found 150 farm animals and pets in the same condition. A woman named Madeline Tolentino added to the mystery in Canóvanas. She said she had seen a bizarre creature walking in the town that day.

Many local people said the killings were the work of a mysterious monster. They called it *chupacabra*, which means "goat sucker." Over the next few years, similar animal deaths happened in parts of the United States and Central and South America.

| **puncture** | a small hole made by a sharp object |

Eyewitnesses describe the chupacabra as 3 to 5 feet (0.9 to 1.5 m) tall.

Some eyewitnesses describe the chupacabra as looking like a lizard or a small dinosaur. Others say it looks like a panther with sharp spines on its back.

Some witnesses claim the chupacabra has glowing red eyes and two small arms with sharp claws.

The chupacabra is said to walk on two legs and hop up to 20 feet (6 m) in a single jump!

eyewitness someone who has seen something take place and can describe what happened

MORE REPORTS

San Germán

Guánica

Cryptozoologists had plenty of eyewitness reports to study in their search for the "goat sucker." People in San Germán, Puerto Rico, claimed they chased away a chupacabra trying to attack some roosters.

In Guánica, Puerto Rico, Osvaldo Claudio Rosado was attacked from behind by a strange and vicious creature. Shortly after the attack, more dead livestock were found.

CHUPACABRA CAPTURED?

07/14/2007

But no one has ever found a chupacabra—or have they? In 2007 Phylis Canion found the bodies of three strange-looking creatures near her ranch in Cuero, Texas. She thought she might finally have proof of the chupacabra's existence.

Scientists at Texas State University-San Marcos studied tissue from the head of one of the creatures. Several months later they made their report. The animal found in Cuero was simply a coyote that had somehow lost its hair.

OTHER POSSIBILITIES

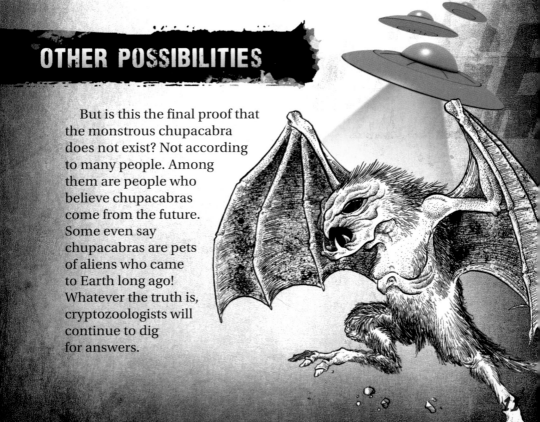

But is this the final proof that the monstrous chupacabra does not exist? Not according to many people. Among them are people who believe chupacabras come from the future. Some even say chupacabras are pets of aliens who came to Earth long ago! Whatever the truth is, cryptozoologists will continue to dig for answers.

BIGFOOT

Height: 8 feet (2.4 m)

Features: walks upright; covered in hair

For centuries stories have been told of apelike creatures wandering through wooded areas of North America. The creature is called "bigfoot" because of its enormous footprint. Hundreds of people claim to have seen one of these beasts.

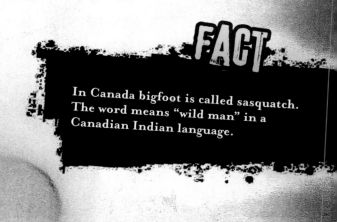

FACT

In Canada bigfoot is called sasquatch. The word means "wild man" in a Canadian Indian language.

Eyewitnesses say bigfoot is about 8 feet (2.4 m) tall.

Bigfoot is covered in shaggy hair. Its hair is usually reported to be brown.

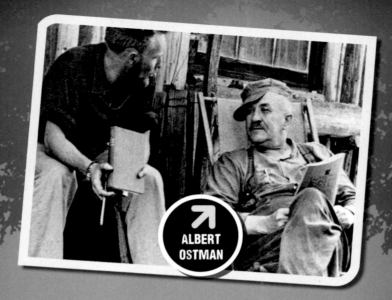

ALBERT OSTMAN

KIDNAPPED BY BIGFOOT?

In 1924 Albert Ostman hiked into the wilderness of British Columbia, Canada, looking for gold. He claimed to have awoke in fear as a huge creature carried him off. Ostman said that when he was finally plopped down, a family of four bigfoots surrounded him. Ostman said he was held captive for six days. He was not harmed. Ostman finally escaped, but he didn't tell his story for 33 years. Ostman said he was afraid people would say he was either crazy or a liar.

 Bigfoot's monstrous footprints usually measure between 15 and 17 inches (40 and 61 cm) long.

 Bigfoot is said to make eerie howls and have a terrible odor.

A bigfoot may actually have been captured on film. In 1967 Roger Patterson and Robert Gimlin were searching for bigfoot near Bluff Creek in California. Suddenly, Patterson claimed he saw one! He grabbed his camera and filmed the beast as it walked away from him. The image Patterson got was blurry and shaky. However, it clearly shows something large and furry looking over its shoulder and then disappearing into the woods. Many people believe that this sighting of bigfoot was a **hoax** created by the two men. No one has ever proven whether the creature on film was bigfoot or a fake.

ISO 800   22

22   22a

STILL FRAME OF THE PATTERSON/GIMLIN FILM

FF CREEK

CALIFORNIA

PACIFIC OCEAN

hoax	a trick or practical joke

THE VERDICT

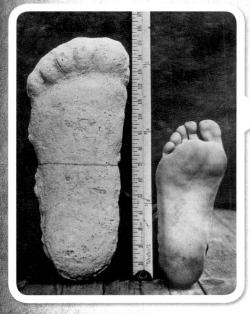

Researchers have a great deal of bigfoot evidence to study. There are plaster casts of footprints, films, photographs, and many eyewitness reports.

Researchers have found unusual hair on brush and trees. There are even animal droppings said to have come from bigfoot.

But until a bigfoot is captured and studied, we won't know if they really exist.

PLASTER CAST OF A BIGFOOT PRINT COMPARED TO A MAN'S FOOT

FACT

In 2004 Bob Heironimus, a friend of Roger Patterson, claimed he was the bigfoot in the film.

THE YETI

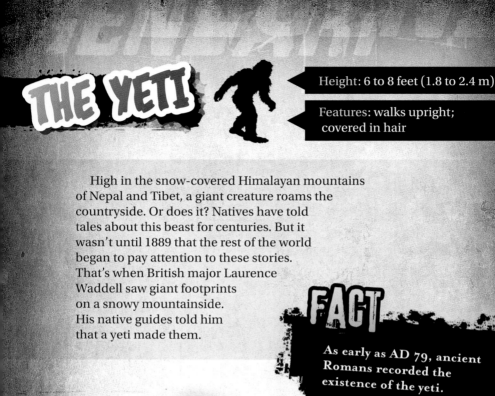

Height: 6 to 8 feet (1.8 to 2.4 m)

Features: walks upright; covered in hair

High in the snow-covered Himalayan mountains of Nepal and Tibet, a giant creature roams the countryside. Or does it? Natives have told tales about this beast for centuries. But it wasn't until 1889 that the rest of the world began to pay attention to these stories. That's when British major Laurence Waddell saw giant footprints on a snowy mountainside. His native guides told him that a yeti made them.

FACT

As early as AD 79, ancient Romans recorded the existence of the yeti.

HIMALAYAN MOUNTAINS

12–13 inches (30.5–33 cm)

In 1951 a group led by British mountaineer Eric Shipton came upon a set of large footprints. Photographs show that the prints appeared to have been made by a large apelike animal.

In 1954 a team of British researchers went in search of the beast. They excitedly returned with hairs from what they believed was a yeti. Professor Frederick Woods Jones studied the hair. He could not tell what type of animal it had come from. He did believe, however, that the hair probably came from a hoofed animal, and not a yeti. To this day, there is no solid proof that the yeti exists.

THE BEAST OF GÉVAUDAN

Height: 6 feet (1.8 m)

Features: sharp teeth; long claws

FRENCH COUNTRYSIDE ↗

Beginning in 1764, in Gévaudan, France, a series of ferocious animal attacks occurred. The guilty predator killed more than 100 people. Most of the victims were women and children. Many residents were convinced that a werewolf was on the loose.

WHAT WAS IT?

Descriptions of the beast varied. Some witnesses claimed it was a wolflike predator. Others claimed it was more like a hyena or a cat.

GREY WOLF

BLACK PANTHER

STRIPED HYENA

Still others said it was a hoofed animal. Most witnesses agreed that it was as large as a donkey, had red-tinted brown fur, and small ears.

The beast was not shy. It killed in broad daylight, often leaving witnesses behind to describe the attacks. The beast seemed to pounce out of nowhere. It often attacked a victim's throat.

The French king sent out large hunting parties to kill the beast. The hunters killed several wolves they thought were the beast. But the attacks continued.

THE MYSTERY REMAINS

People have had many theories about what the beast of Gévaudan was. Some investigators believe it was a hyena that was either wild or trained to kill by its owner. Others think the beast was a cross between a wolf and a dog. Still others believe it was a prehistoric animal that had survived to modern times. When considering the frequency and distance between attacks, it is also likely that there was more than one beast. Whatever the beast was, its attacks stopped in 1767. But its victims are proof that something mysterious was indeed roaming through France in the 1760s.

MOKELE-MBEMBE

Height: 5 to 6 feet (1.5 to 1.8 m)

Length: 10.8 to 16.5 feet (3.3 to 5 m)

CONGO, AFRICA

Take a trip down the Congo River in Africa, and you may see one of the last surviving dinosaurs. Cryptozoologist Roy Mackal believes a dinosaur-like animal lurks in the jungles near this river. In 1980 and 1981 Mackal went in search of the monster that natives call mokele-mbembe (mo-KEH-lay-muhm-BEH).

For hundreds of years, the beast had been spoken of in local folklore. It was said to be the size of an elephant with a long, flexible neck and a long tail. There had also been footprint sightings and eyewitness reports of the animal.

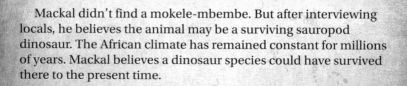

Mackal didn't find a mokele-mbembe. But after interviewing locals, he believes the animal may be a surviving sauropod dinosaur. The African climate has remained constant for millions of years. Mackal believes a dinosaur species could have survived there to the present time.

Sauropods were a group of dinosaurs that included many species. Some sauropods grew up to 100 ft (30.5 m) long. Common features unite all sauropods.

plant eater	small head	long neck	five toes	long tail

MONSTER OF THE AMAZON: CASE SOLVED?

A THREE-TOED SLOTH ➡️

Deep in the rainforest of South America, tales are told of the frightening mapinguary, or "roaring animal." Eyewitnesses claim the beast has thick, matted fur. They say it is over 7 feet (2.1 m) tall when it stands on its rear legs. Its tracks and snout are similar of those of a sloth. The awful smell of the animal is said to be so strong that it causes dizziness and fainting. Many natives believe that a mapinguary killed a large group of cattle in 1937. All of the animals had their tongues ripped out. Scientist David Oren has studied the mapinguary. He believes that the creature might be a relative of the mylodon. This giant sloth died out more than 10,000 years ago. Smaller sloths are known to still exist in South America.

sloth	a mammal with long arms and legs, curved claws, and a shaggy coat

UP FROM THE
WATERY DEPTHS

Throughout the world, eyewitnesses have reported strange sightings in bodies of water. Investigators have a hard time knowing what a water-dwelling creature looks like. Eyewitness reports often differ. Witnesses have nothing to compare a creature's size to. This can lead to difficulties in estimating a creature's height and length.

LOCH NESS MONSTER

Length: 10 to 45 feet (3 m to 14 m)

Features: long neck; small head

FACT

Ninety percent of the Earth's living space is in the oceans. Very little of this area has been explored by humans.

SCOTLAND

LOCH NESS

GREAT BRITAIN

Loch Ness in Scotland may be home to the world's most famous mystery creature. The Loch Ness monster is also known as "Nessie." Thousands of sightings of the creature have been reported.

Nessie is said to have a small head and a long neck.

Nessie has at least one hump on its back. Some witnesses claim to have seen more than one hump.

10 to 45 feet (3 m to 14 m)

One reason behind the differing descriptions of Nessie may be that people aren't seeing a lake monster at all. They may be seeing seals, otters, or tree limbs in the water.

SEAL

NESSIE SIGHTINGS AND SEARCHES TIMELINE

Color film of Nessie is taken by G. E. Taylor.

 sonar
 audio
 eyewitness
 film

 1933

1960

1938

April: John Mackay and his wife reported seeing a large black body with two humps in the lake.

July: George Spicer and his wife claimed Nessie crossed the road in front of their car. The couple said it looked like the monster was carrying a lamb in its mouth.

Tim Dinsdale took the most famous film of Nessie. British Air Force researchers said it shows a creature 12 to 16 feet (3.7 to 4.9 m) long.

 FACT

According to legend, the first Nessie sighting was in 565 by Saint Columba.

STAINED GLASS IMAGE OF ST. COLUMBA ←

Using **sonar** and an underwater camera, Dr. Robert Rhines detected what appeared to be flipper movement from a large animal.

Sonar readings aboard the ship M. V. *Nessie Hunter* showed a snakelike shape with two humps.

1995

2000

2003

1972

In 1995 and 2000, underwater microphones recorded unexplained animal sounds that might have been made by Nessie.

2001

A team of scientists used sonar to scan Loch Ness and found no evidence of Nessie's existence.

Many photos and videos have supposedly captured Nessie. Researchers have also taken many sonar readings of large unknown objects in Loch Ness. But no concrete evidence for Nessie's existence has ever been found.

Some cryptozoologists believe Nessie might be a surviving dinosaur. Others claim Nessie might be an unknown mammal or **amphibian**. Still others believe it is a very large eel. Of course, it may also be just a figment of the imagination.

sonar	an instrument used to calculate how deep water is or where underwater objects are
amphibian	a cold-blooded animal with a backbone; amphibians live in water when young and can live on land as adults

CHAMP

Length: 12 to 75 feet (3.7 to 23 m)

Features: long neck; small head

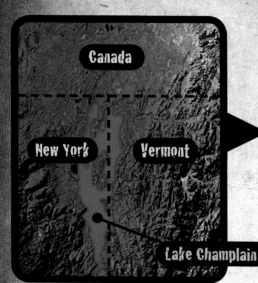

Canada

New York

Vermont

Lake Champlain

Lake Champlain is located on the New York and Vermont border. For centuries, people have reported seeing a giant sea monster in the lake. Locals call the monster "Champ."

Champ has been reported to be anywhere from 12 to 75 feet (3.7 to 23 m) long. It is dark in color with rough skin. Its neck is reported to be 5 to 8 feet (1.5 to 2.4 m) long. Most reports say it has three humps on its back.

EVIDENCE OF CHAMP

In 1979 sonar detected a large underwater object in the lake. It was traveling 175 feet (53 m) below the lake's surface.

In 2005 a video appeared on YouTube that convinced many people of Champ's existence. But some reviewers claimed they couldn't see any object at all.

MAKING WAVES

A seiche is a wave that can occur in water that is bound by land on all sides. A small example of a seiche would be waves you make in the bathtub. Long, deep lakes often have seiches. Lake Champlain and Loch Ness are two lakes that have such waves. Seiches can drag material from the bottom of a lake back up to the surface. Debris travels along the bottom of the lake until it reaches a point where it pops back up. These happenings could account for some of the Champ and Nessie sightings.

FACT

Cryptozoologist Roy Mackal thinks Champ could be a surviving zeuglodon. This type of whale died out more than 20 million years ago. Zeuglodon fossils have been found near Lake Champlain.

The strongest evidence of Champ's existence may be a photo taken by Sandra Mansi in 1977. Experts and cryptozoologists who studied the photo said it was not a fake. Cryptozoologist Paul LeBlond said the creature in the picture could have been as large as 60 feet (18.3 m) long. But others say the object is simply a floating tree limb.

THE KRAKEN

Length: up to 1.5 miles (2.4 km)

Features: large tentacles

In the 1200s sailors near Norway and Iceland began to see gigantic squid-like creatures. They called these creatures krakens.

Over the years, sailors reported seeing these creatures fiercely attack ships. Late in the 1700s, a Danish ship was reportedly attacked by a kraken off the coast of West Africa. The captain said that a giant sea creature grabbed and killed three of his crewmen. He estimated the beast's **tentacles** were 35 feet (10.7 m) long.

Many kraken reports were almost beyond belief. The kraken's body was supposedly 1.5 miles (2.4 km) around. It was so big that it looked like small islands surrounded by seaweed. Because of these exaggerations and lack of proof, most scientists believed the kraken was a myth.

tentacle   a long, flexible arm of an animal

FACT

The myth of the kraken is kept alive in movies such as *Pirates of the Caribbean.*

French scientist Pierre Denys de Montfort took the stories of the kraken seriously. For years he interviewed whale hunters. They told him eerie stories of giant creatures attacking ships and killing sailors. In 1802 de Montfort wrote that he believed such creatures existed. Other scientists made fun of his beliefs.

PROOF OF THE KRAKEN

In the 1870s people began taking the kraken seriously. The bodies of large, tentacle-covered sea creatures were found washed up on the shores of Newfoundland, Canada.

In 1878 the body of one of the beasts measured 20 feet (6.1 m) long. Its largest tentacle was 35 feet (10.7 m) long. That put its total length at 55 feet (16.8 m)!

After many years, de Montfort was proven right. The mythical beast known as the kraken was actually the very real giant squid. Another type of squid was also discovered. The colossal squid grows nearly as long as the giant squid and weighs even more.

DISCOVERIES CONTINUE

In the late 1800s, the bodies of giant squid washed ashore all over the world. Sightings continue to this day.

1880

A 65-foot (19.8–m) giant squid washed up in New Zealand.

THE BLOOP:
MYSTERY SOUND OF THE DEEP

During the 1960s the U.S. military set up a system of underwater microphones. At the time, the microphones were used to track enemy submarines. In the 1990s the U.S. government donated the microphone system to scientists to track ocean activity. In 1997 two microphones 3,000 miles (4,828 km) apart picked up the same bizarre sound. Scientists have since named the sound the bloop. The bloop shared similarities with whale sounds, but it was much louder. No known animal is large enough to make a sound so loud. Some scientists believe the sound was made by a gigantic sea creature yet to be discovered.

The lusca is said to lurk in deep underwater caves near the Bahamas. The beast is described as half octopus, half shark. According to witnesses, it is 50 feet (15 m) wide and has tentacles with sucker tips.

COLOSSAL SQUID (2007)

1968 A 100-foot (30–m) squid was seen on the water's surface near Puerto Rico.

2007 A fishing crew accidentally caught a colossal squid off the coast of Antarctica. The creature weighed nearly 1,000 pounds (454 kg)!

THE BEAST OF 'BUSCO

Length: 7 to 10 feet (2.1 to 3 m)

Features: hard shell; short limbs

In 1898 Oscar Fulk of Churubusco, Indiana, reported seeing an enormous turtle in the lake on his family farm. No one believed him.

By 1948 Gale Harris owned the Fulk farm. Harris let two local fishermen use the lake on his property. They came back with a tall tale about a giant turtle. Not only did Harris believe them, he claimed to have seen the turtle himself.

The turtle was described as 7 to 10 feet (2.1 to 3 m) long and 5 feet (1.5) wide. Witnesses compared the size of the turtle's shell to a car.

HUNTING THE BEAST

Soon newspaper and TV reporters picked up the story of the beast of 'Busco. They nicknamed the turtle Oscar. Harris made it his mission to prove that Oscar was real. Thousands of people crowded the Harris property hoping to get a glimpse of Oscar.

 Harris built homemade turtle traps. He even used a female turtle as bait.

 Divers were sent to the depths of the lake to search out Oscar.

Eventually, Harris had nearly all of the water pumped out of the lake. Some people claimed to have seen the turtle at this point. But there was never any proof.

 ALLIGATOR SNAPPING TURTLE

OSCAR MYSTERY SOLVED?

If Oscar existed, he might have been a large alligator snapping turtle. These turtles have been known to reach 220 pounds (100 kg). They are usually about 2 feet (.6 m) long, but it may be possible for them to grow larger. Alligator snapping turtles usually live south of Indiana, but they do move north as they age. These turtles commonly live 50 to 100 years. Perhaps we'll hear more reports of Oscar yet.

THEY COME FROM THE SKIES!

OWLMAN

Length: 7 feet (2.1 m)

Features: part owl; part man; red eyes

In 1976 weird things began happening in the town of Mawnan, England. Wild birds attacked some people. Other people claimed to see UFOs. But strangest of all, people reported seeing a bizarre flying creature.

The creature looked like an owl, but it had long legs and was larger than a human. Witnesses also claimed the beast had red eyes.

Several witnesses said the owlman was perched on the Mawnan church tower.

"I saw this monster bird last night. It stood like a man then it flew up though the trees. It is as big as a man. Its eyes are red and shine brightly." Sally Chapman 4/7/76

The first owlman sighting happened in April 1976. Two young girls, June and Vicky Melling, reported seeing a large "bird-man" flying over a church. In July two more girls, Sally Chapman and Barbara Perry, saw the creature. They described it as having gray feathers and black, clawed feet. They also said it had a "nasty owl face with big ears and big red eyes." Over the next two years, more sightings of the owlman were reported.

OWLMAN OR JUST AN OWL?

It's possible that the owlman was actually a Eurasian eagle owl. This owl is the largest known type of owl. An eagle owl can be 2.5 feet (.8 m) tall and have a wingspan of up to 6.5 feet (2 m). As its name implies, the Eurasian eagle owl is found in parts of Europe and Asia. But England is not part of its normal territory. Could the owlman have been an owl who'd lost its way?

KONGAMATO

In the early 1900s, explorer Frank Melland was working in southern Africa. Natives told him about a creature that had large teeth, red or black skin, and a wingspan of 4 to 7 feet (1.2 to 2.1 m). The beast lived in local swamps. It often attacked people on the water. For this reason, the native people called the creature *kongamato*, which means "breaker of boats."

PTEROSAURS

When African natives were shown drawings of a pterosaur, they claimed it looked exactly like the kongamato. Pterosaurs were featherless flying reptiles that lived from 65 to 251 million years ago. They could be as small as a lemon or as large as a small airplane. Pterosaurs had a mouthful of sharp pointed teeth used for catching fish.

In 1988 cryptozoologist Roy Mackal went to southern Africa. He found ostrich bones on high hilltops. Mackal believed that a huge, powerful creature carried the ostriches into the air.

Most researchers say that witnesses mistake other types of large birds for the kongamato. Several species of giant storks live in southern Africa.

SHOEBILL STORK

But some cryptozoologists think the kongamato is a surviving pterosaur. After all, fossils of flying reptiles have been found in the region. These fossils look much like the reports of kongamatos.

The African swamps are wild, overgrown areas. They are nearly impossible for humans to explore. Perhaps they are hiding a prehistoric secret.

SADDLE-BILLED STORK

THUNDERBIRD

Wingspan: between 36 and 160 feet (11 and 49 m)

Features: featherless; large wingspan

For centuries, Native Americans told stories of a giant bird. This creature could cause storms with the flapping of its wings. The creature was so powerful that it could carry off big prey like deer. They called this beast "thunderbird."

On April 26, 1890, the thunderbird made the headlines of the Tombstone, Arizona, *Epitaph*. An article in the newspaper reported that two cowboys on horseback chased a winged monster. They eventually shot and killed it. The men said the bird looked like a giant alligator with wings. They claimed the animal was 92 feet (28 m) long and had a 160-foot (49–m) wingspan.

There is also an interesting photograph from the 1800s. It shows U.S. soldiers surrounding what appears to be a dead winged beast. The animal in this photo appears to have a wingspan of 36 feet (11 m). To this day, no one knows if the photo goes with the original story or if either was a hoax.

CALIFORNIA CONDORS

California condors are a bird species living in the western United States. They can grow up to 4.4 feet (1.3 m) long and have a 9-foot (2.7-m) wingspan. When Native Americans spoke of the thunderbird, they were usually referring to this bird. However, some of the thunderbird reports described it as far too large to be a California condor.

In 1972 another explanation for the existence of the thunderbird surfaced. The fossilized remains of a gigantic pterosaur were discovered in southwest Texas. Is it possible a relative of this enormous prehistoric beast still roams the skies of the United States?

MOTHMAN

Between November 1966 and November 1967, a winged creature was reported flying near Point Pleasant, West Virginia. The strangest sighting came from four people riding together in a car. They said they saw a 6– or 7–foot (1.8– or 2.1–m) tall monster with glowing red eyes. The driver took off. But the creature chased the car at speeds up to 100 miles (161 km) per hour!

The creature's wingspan was reported at 6 to 10 feet (1.8 to 3 m).

Witnesses claimed the beast had large red eyes that glowed in the dark.

Soon the town of Point Pleasant
was in a frenzy over the creature.
The beast was nicknamed "Mothman"
by newspaper and TV reporters.

Mothman often
appeared shortly before
or after other strange
events. Doors would
open or close on their
own. People even reported
seeing UFOs or odd lights
in the sky at the same time
as Mothman sightings.

Some people believed
Mothman was a warning
of coming disasters. About
a year after the Mothman
sightings began, a local bridge
collapsed. Forty-six people
were killed as a result. After the
bridge collapse, the Mothman
sightings stopped.

Skeptics believe that the
mysterious Mothman was just a
large owl. At the other extreme are people
who think Mothman was an ultraterrestrial
being. Ultraterrestrials are beings that have
developed on Earth in another **dimension**
that humans cannot see.

dimension   the position of an object
in space and time

41

CHAPTER 4

FAMOUS MONSTER HOAXES AND
FUTURE POSSIBILITIES

THE DOCTOR AND THE MERMAID

In July 1842 a man going by the name Dr. J. Griffin showed up in New York City. He brought with him the body of a mermaid. It was supposedly caught near the Fiji Islands in the South Pacific Ocean. Dr. Griffin displayed the mermaid at Concert Hall on Broadway. Later, circus manager P. T. Barnum convinced Griffin to show the mermaid at his museum.

But the joke was on the people who paid to see the creature. The "mermaid" was simply the upper body of a monkey sewn onto the body of a fish! The "doctor" turned out to be Levi Lyman. Barnum had hired Lyman to be part of the hoax.

FACT

Barnum is credited for saying, "There's a sucker born every minute."

THE STONE GIANT

People in Cardiff, New York, were in for a big shock in 1869. Workers drilling a well on George Newell's farm discovered a rock giant. The huge stone man was 10 feet, 4.5 inches (3.2 meters) tall and weighed nearly 3,000 pounds (1,361 kg). Thousands of people flocked to the small town. They paid fifty cents to see what they believed was either a fossil of a giant man or an ancient statue.

In 1870 a Yale science professor took a closer look at the giant. He said it was neither a fossil nor a valuable ancient statue. Instead, he said it was a crude carving. Eventually, a man named George Hull admitted he had created the entire hoax. Two years earlier, Hull had the giant carved from a block of stone and buried in the ground. He made more than $30,000 from his sneaky plan.

123

43

THE HUNT CONTINUES

Despite hoaxes, cryptozoologists continue to search for legendary monsters. Their past work has revealed that many bizarre creatures live among us. Will cryptozoologists ever find a living bigfoot or chupacabra?

GORILLA OR BIGFOOT?

COYOTE OR CHUPACABRA?

OKAPI: THE AFRICAN UNICORN

African natives have known about the okapi for hundreds of years. This four-legged creature looks like a donkey with the legs and hind end of a zebra. Its tongue is long enough to lick its eyelids. To the Europeans exploring Africa in the 1800s, this animal sounded too strange to be real. They joked that the okapi was just a myth—the African version of the unicorn. But in 1901, explorer Sir Harry Johnston discovered an okapi for himself. The animal turned out to be related to giraffes. Today about 30,000 exist. About 5,000 of them live in the Okapi Wildlife Reserve in central Africa.

Will research at Loch Ness finally prove the existence of Nessie? Could Nessie and Champ be the same type of beast?

BUZZARD OR THUNDERBIRD?

NESSIE OR DRIFTWOOD?

FACT

The coelacanth, a prehistoric fish, had been thought to be extinct for millions of years. In 1938 these fish were found alive and well, swimming off the coast of Africa.

With so much to discover, who can say that we won't find a yeti walking over snow-covered mountains? Maybe someone will capture a kongamato as it soars through the African skies. Scientists will continue to explore the existence of these bizarre creatures. Until they find proof, you can decide what you believe for yourself.

GLOSSARY

amphibian (am-FI-bee-uhn)—cold-blooded animal with a backbone; amphibians live in water when young and can live on land as adults

dimension (dih-MEN-shun)—the location of an object in space and time

eyewitness (eye-WIT-ness)—someone who has seen something occur and can describe what happened

fossil (FOSS-uhl)—the remains of an animal or plant, preserved as rock

hoax (HOHKS)—a trick or practical joke

predator (PRED-uh-tur)—an animal that hunts other animals for food

puncture (PUHNGK-chur)—a hole made by a sharp object

sloth (SLOTH)—a tree-dwelling mammal with long arms and legs and a shaggy coat

sonar (SOH-nar)—an instrument used to determine where underwater objects are

species (SPEE-sheez)—a group of animals or plants that share common characteristics

tentacle (TEN-tuh-kuhl)—a long, flexible arm of an animal

READ MORE

Halls, Kelly Milner, and Rick Spears. *Tales of the Cryptids: Mysterious Creatures that May or May Not Exist.* Plain City, Ohio: Darby Creek Publishing, 2006.

Miller, Karen. *Monsters and Water Beasts: Creatures of Fact or Fiction?* New York: Henry Holt & Company, 2007.

Teitelbaum, Michael. *Bigfoot Caught on Film: and Other Monster Sightings!* 24/7: Science Behind the Scenes. New York: Franklin Watts, 2008.

INTERNET SITES

FactHound offers a safe, fun way to find Internet sites related to this book. All of the sites on FactHound have been researched by our staff.

Here's all you do:

Visit *www.facthound.com*

Type in this code: 9781429648172